A Sunshine Garden Doll Pattern

Sage

By Anne Cote

Sage

**For more Sunshine Garden Dolls Patterns
Visit bluedaisyzone.com**

Daisy

Sunflower

Poppy   Dandelion   Marigold   Rosemary   Sage   Primrose

ISBN-13: 978-1-940354-69-9

Text, Photos, and Illustrations by Anne Cote
Cover Design by Anne Cote & Layne Walker
Edited by Joan Cote and Layne Walker

First edition published in January 2021
Published by New Friends Publishing, LLC
Lake Havasu City, AZ

Visit New Friends Publishing's Website at
www.newfriendspublishing.com

CONTENTS

To

All Gardeners

who Love to Grow

Beautiful and Beneficial Plants

Materials for Sage

Sage is a bright, happy-go-lucky boy. He likes to play in the garden among the herbs. He always has fun picking flowers for his twin sister, Rosemary (pattern sold separately). Sage is 20" tall. He rolls up his sleeves and overalls when he gets down to business in the garden.

SUPPLIES

There are lots of options for materials, including scraps of fabric and fancy trims. I've listed the products I use in brackets. Other options abound and are listed below.

DOLL

44"x13" cotton fabric for body
Craft paint, markers
    [Anita's White for whites of eyes and dots in the eyes]
    [Sharpie Permanent Markers for eyes, nose, brows, lashes, mouth]
Yarn for hair [Yarn Bee Snuggle Up: "Black"]
Poly-fil Stuffing 6-8 oz.
Glue for the hair
Stuffing tools [tube and stick]
Fabric turning tools [tube and stick, see instructions]

CLOTHING

18"x15" cotton fabric for shirt
26"x15" denim or cotton fabric for overalls
12"x8" black felt for shoes

4 snap fasteners (2 for shirt, 2 for overalls)
General sewing supplies

OPTIONS

Face can be painted, embroidered, or drawn on with permanent markers.
Hair instructions are for gluing on the yarn. Hand sewing can be used instead, or a combination of hand sewing and glue.
Snaps can be plastic or metal or replaced by buttons.

COPYRIGHT and CHILD SAFETY

COPYRIGHT

What **CAN** you do? You **CAN** sell the items that you make from this pattern. You can use the templates to create the doll. You can also add your own artistic flare to what you create when using the templates. What you make is your property and is yours to do with as you wish.

What **CAN'T** you do? You **CANNOT** copy the pattern illustrations, diagrams, written instructions or photos. You cannot simply photocopy, scan, or reproduce the sewing pattern in any way and then sell copies of it. This is an infringement of copyright laws.

CHILD SAFETY

This doll is advised for children 3 years or older. For a younger child or baby, bows, sashes, ribbons, or any loose parts should be removed or sewn securely onto the doll or clothing. Fancy laces can wear out with use and separate from the clothing. They are preferable for children over 3. Plastic baby snaps can be used instead of metal snaps. The pattern calls for painting the face. Embroidery and painting are safety measures. Buttons should not be used for eyes for small children. I cannot be responsible for the way each crafter uses these patterns or instructions. Please consider the age of the child for which you are making the doll.

For more information on copyright laws and safety information, there is a great amount of information on the internet. For pattern questions, please send an email to Anne at this address: bluedaisyzone@gmail.com

Making the Doll

All seam allowances are 1/4 inch.

Use a small machine stich for more stability.

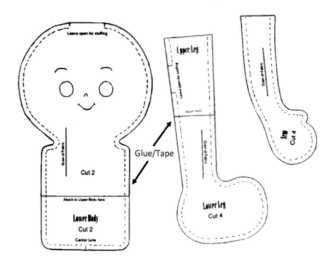

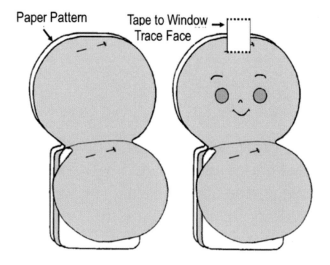

Cut out the patterns. Glue or tape the leg and body pieces together where indicated. Pin to fabric and cut out pieces.

FACE: Lay the fabric head/body on top of the paper pattern. Pin one side of the fabric head to the pattern top. Pin the folded layer of fabric to the lower body. Tape or hold the head/body to a window or lightbox and trace the face with pencil.

All the features can be painted or embroidered. For Sage, I used Sharpie Permanent Markers for all the features except for the white acrylic paint for the whites of the eyes and the dots on the eyes.

Sage's eyes, lashes, and brows are black. His nose can be black or dark brown. His mouth is red.

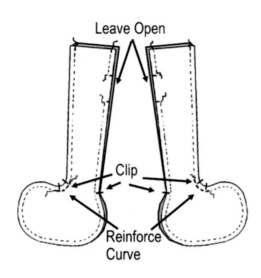

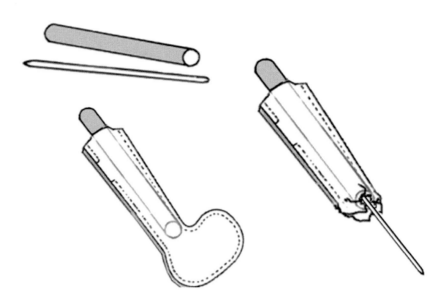

LEGS: Right sides together, stitch the legs, leaving the opening in the upper section for stuffing. Reinforce the curve between the top of the foot and leg. Clip curves.

Turn the legs right side out. My favorite way of turning narrow fabric pieces is with a tube and stick. In this case, push the tube inside the leg. With the stick, push the foot into the tube until it comes out the other end.

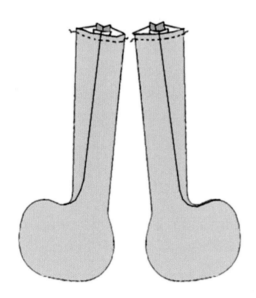

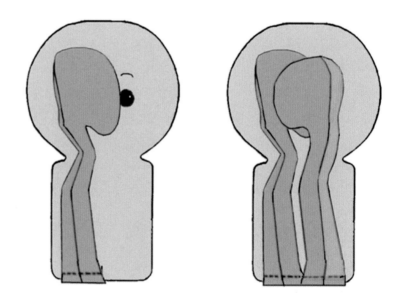

Open the top of the legs and pin the seams together. Baste across the top.

Place the top of the legs on the bottom of the right side of the body with the face. It's very important that the toes face the features on the face. Otherwise, the feet and legs will come out backwards. The leg tops should lie 1/4 inch from the side of the body on both sides. The legs should hang just below the body about 1/8 inch to make sure they are caught in the stitches. The legs might overlap a little in the middle. Pin/baste the legs in place along the bottom of the body.

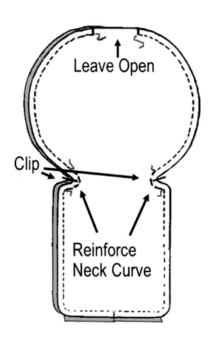

Leave Open

Clip

Reinforce
Neck Curve

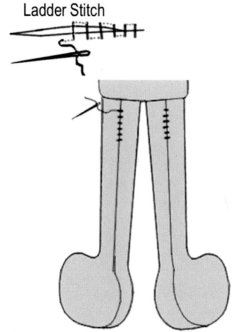

Ladder Stitch

BODY: Right sides together, pin/baste the entire body, making sure the feet and legs are not caught in the seam allowance. Starting at the head, stitch around the entire body, leaving the opening for the stuffing. Reinforce the neck area with extra stitches. Clip the curves.

Turn the body right side out. Stuff the body and head. Sew the head closed with a ladder stitch as shown above.

On the back side, stuff the legs. Close the legs with a ladder stitch.

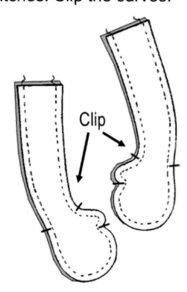

Clip

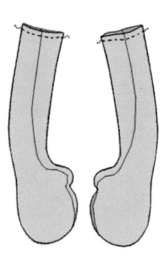

Overcast Stitch

ARMS: Right sides together, stitch the arms. Clip curves. Turn right side out.

Stuff the arms to about 1 inch from the top. Turn the top edge inside 1/4 inch and pin closed. Hand sew or machine stitch closed.

Pin arms to shoulders. Stitch by hand with an overcast stitch.

Making the Hair

Please read all the instructions before starting the hair.

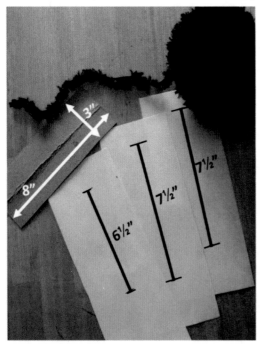

2. Wrap the yarn 50 times around the 3-inch side of the cardboard. The width of the yarn should stretch 7½ inches across the cardboard.

3. Place a piece masking tape across the top of the yarn about ½ inch on both sides. Do not cut the yarn.

1. Preparation: For the hair, use the long side of three half-sheets of copy paper. (You can use stabilizer material instead if you wish.) Draw a 7½-inch line down the middle of two pieces of paper. Draw a 6½-inch line down the other piece. These lines will be a guide for the length of the seams that hold the yarn together. For wrapping the yarn, you will need a piece of lightweight cardboard that is 3 inches wide by at least 8 inches long. The cardboard should be lightweight enough to crease down the middle of the long side.

4. Fold the cardboard slightly and carefully slide the yarn off the cardboard. Move the yarn to one of the papers with a 7½-inch line. Line up the center of the yarn with the line. .

5. Stitch the yarn half-way between the tape. Help push the yarn under the pressure foot as the stitches are made. Use a small stitch to make more perforations in the paper, making it easier to remove. After sewing, remove the tape and the paper.

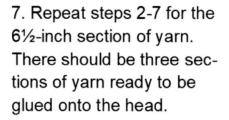

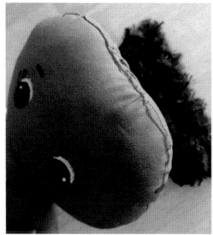

6. Repeat steps 2 to 7 to make another 7½-inch section of yarn.

7. Repeat steps 2-7 for the 6½-inch section of yarn. There should be three sections of yarn ready to be glued onto the head.

8. **6½-inch section**: With a pen or marker, make a line about 1 inch down one side of the head to 1 inch down the other side. This line should be about 1/4 inch in front of the seam on the head. Place a line of glue over this line and attach the 6½-inch section of yarn.

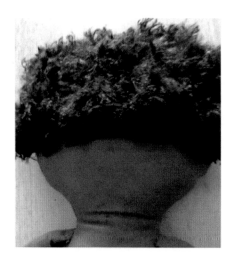

9. **7½-inch section 1**: Make a line from one side of the head to the other side about 1 inch below the hair. Place a line of glue over this line as well as some dots of glue just above it and below it. Attach the first 7½-inch section of yarn.

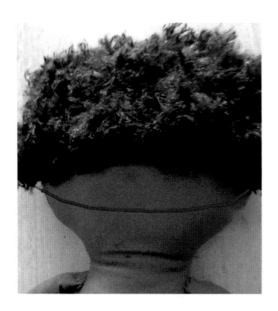

10. **7½-inch section 2**: Make a curved line from one side of the head to the other side, dipping about 1 inch below the hair. Place a line of glue over this line as well as dots of glue just above it and below it. Attach the second 7½-inch section of yarn. Sage is ready to dress.

Making the Clothes

All seams are 1/4 inch.

All edges can be finished by using an overstitch or making a tiny fold inward on the edge of the fabric. I use a pinking shears to cut out my pattern pieces and leave this as my finished edge.

Overalls

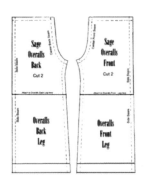

Tape or glue overalls top and bottom pattern pieces together before cutting out the fabric.

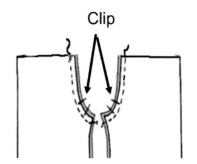

Right sides together, stitch crotch seams front to front and back to back. Clip curves. Press open.

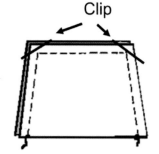

Right sides together, stitch bib on top three sides. Clip corners.

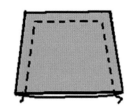

Turn bib right-side out. Top-stitch 1/4 inch from the edge all around the sewn sides.

Pin and baste bib to front of overalls. Stitch bib to overalls 1/4 inch from top edge to hold bib in place.

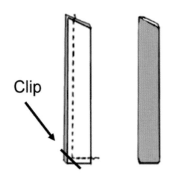

Fold straps over, right sides together. Stitch, leaving diagonal end open. Clip corners. Turn right-side out.

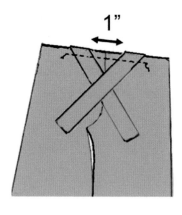

Pin/baste straps to back side of overalls. Line up diagonal edges with top of overalls, leaving 1 inch between straps at the top. Straps should crisscross over each other. Stitch 1/4 inch from top edge to hold straps in place.

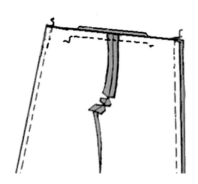

Right sides together, stitch side seams. Press open.

Right sides together, stitch facing seams. Press seams open. Finish bottom edge of facing as desired.

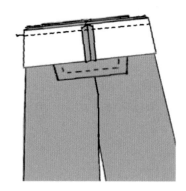

Right sides together, line up facing seams with overalls crotch seams in front and back. Pin/baste facing across waist. Stitch around entire facing 1/4 inch from top.

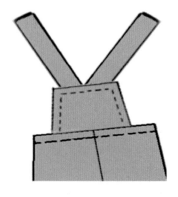

Turn facing to inside. Top-stitch 1/4 inch from edge of waistline around entire front and back.

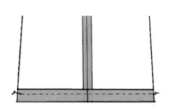

For hem, press lower pant leg up 1/4 inch, then another 1/2 inch. Stitch.

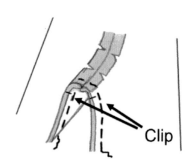

Clip

Right sides together, pin/baste inner pant legs. Stitch from crotch seam to hem on each side. Clip curves at crotch. Press seams open. Turn overalls right-side out.

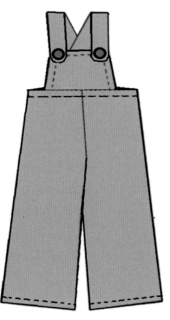

Attach snaps to straps and bib.

Shirt

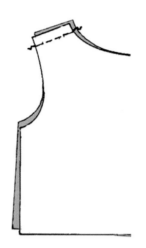

Right sides together, stitch shoulder seams on shirt bodice. Press open.

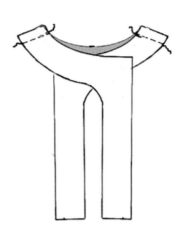

Right sides together, stitch shoulder seams on facing. Press open.

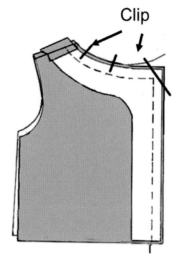

Right sides together, pin/baste facing to bodice. Stitch around entire facing. Clip curves. Clip corners.

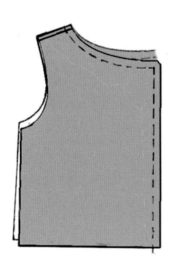

Turn facing to inside. Press. Top-stitch close to edge around entire front sides and neck.

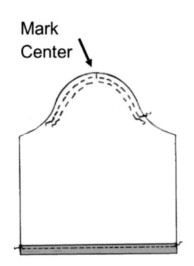

Mark center of sleeve cap. Sew two rows of running stitches over sleeve cap. Press lower edge under 1/4 inch, then another 1/4 inch to form hem. Stitch.

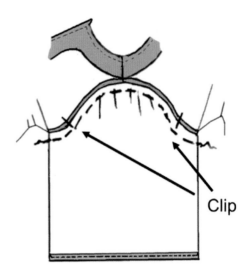

Right sides together, match center of sleeve to shoulder seam. Pull up gathering threads to fit armhole. Pin/baste sleeve to armhole and stitch. Clip curves.

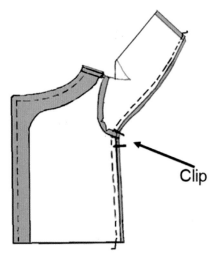

Clip

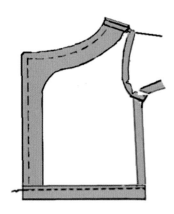

Right sides together, pin/baste side seams. Seam allowance of armhole should be sewn toward sleeve. Stitch from bottom of bodice to end of sleeve. Clip curves. Press seam open.

To form bodice hem, press raw edge to wrong side 1/4 inch, then another 1/4 inch. Stitch.

For boys, the left front should overlap the right front. For girls, the right front should overlap the left front. Attach snaps.

Shoes

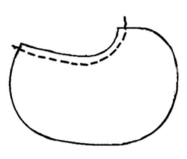

On each shoe piece, stay-stitch along top edge for stability.

Reinforce

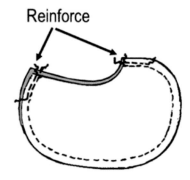

With right sides together, stitch from toe to back of heel. Reinforce beginning and ending with extra stitches for stability.

Patterns
For
Doll and Clothing

Patterns can be cut out or traced.

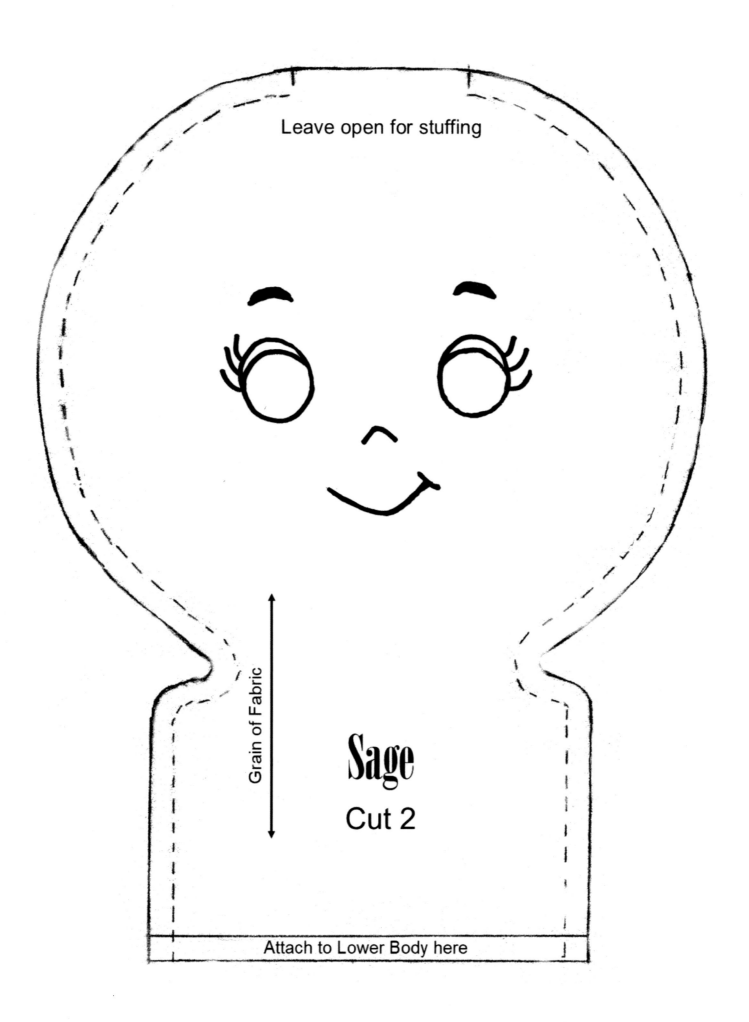

Leave open for stuffing

Grain of Fabric

Sage

Cut 2

Attach to Lower Body here

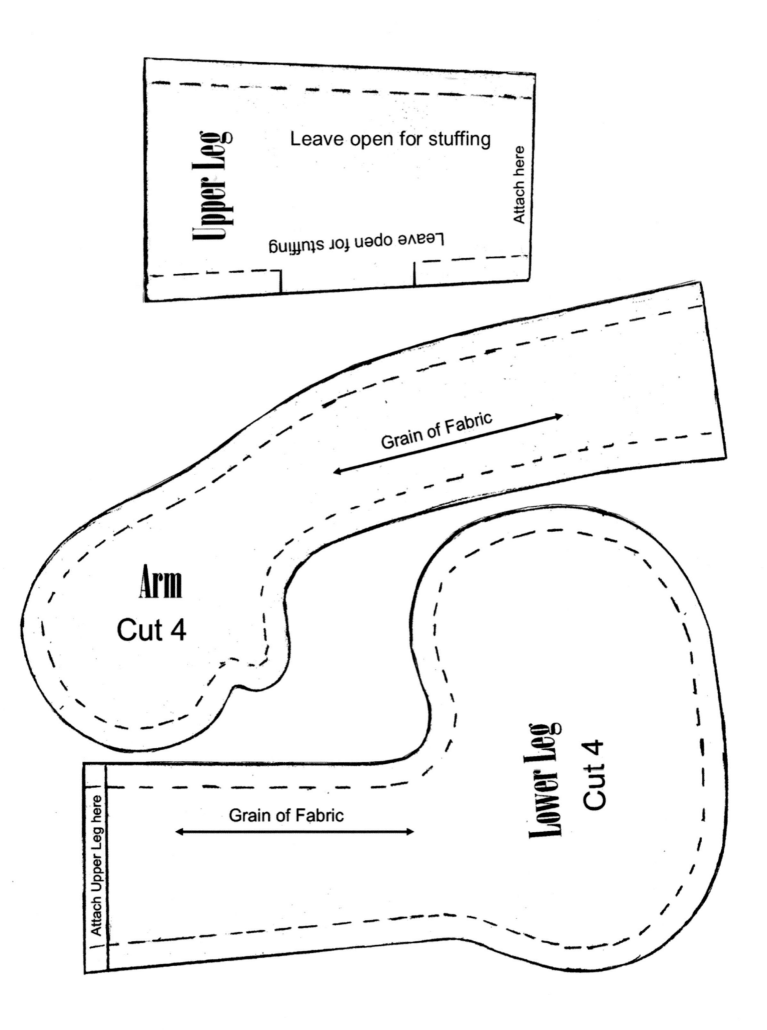

Upper Leg

Leave open for stuffing

Leave open for stuffing

Attach here

Grain of Fabric

Arm
Cut 4

Lower Leg
Cut 4

Grain of Fabric

Attach Upper Leg here

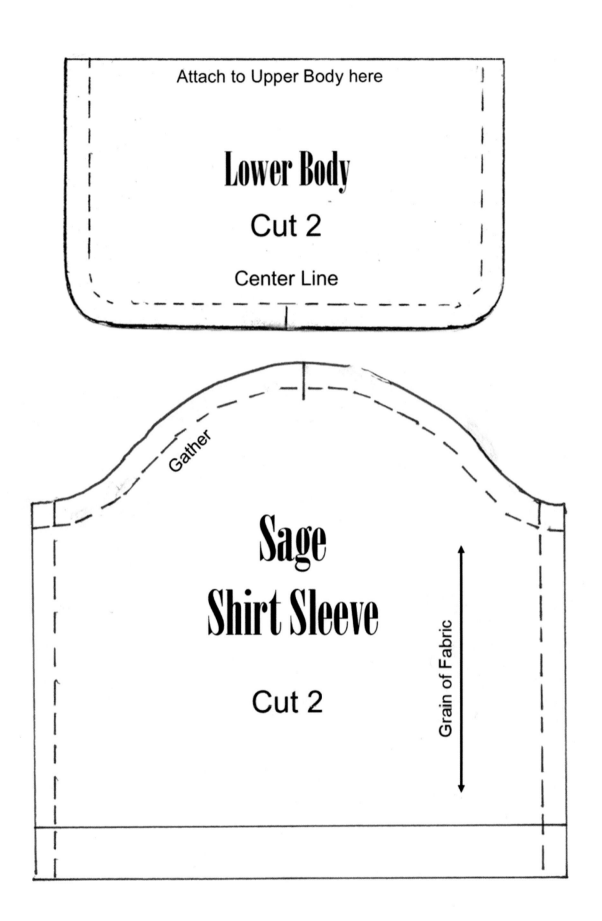

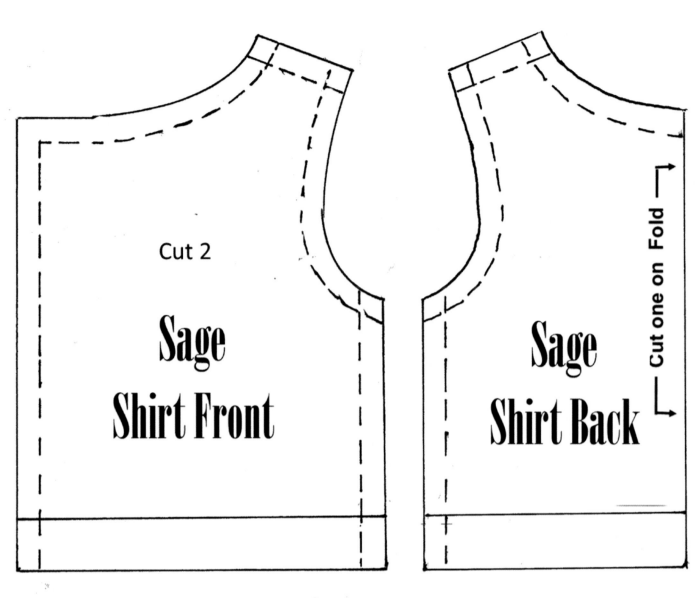

Cut 2

Sage
Shirt Front

Sage
Shirt Back

Cut one on Fold →

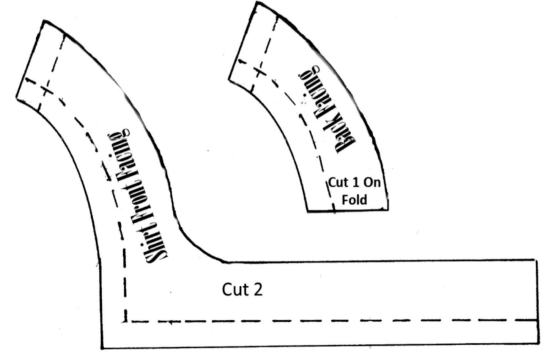

Shirt Front Facing

Back Facing

Cut 1 On Fold

Cut 2

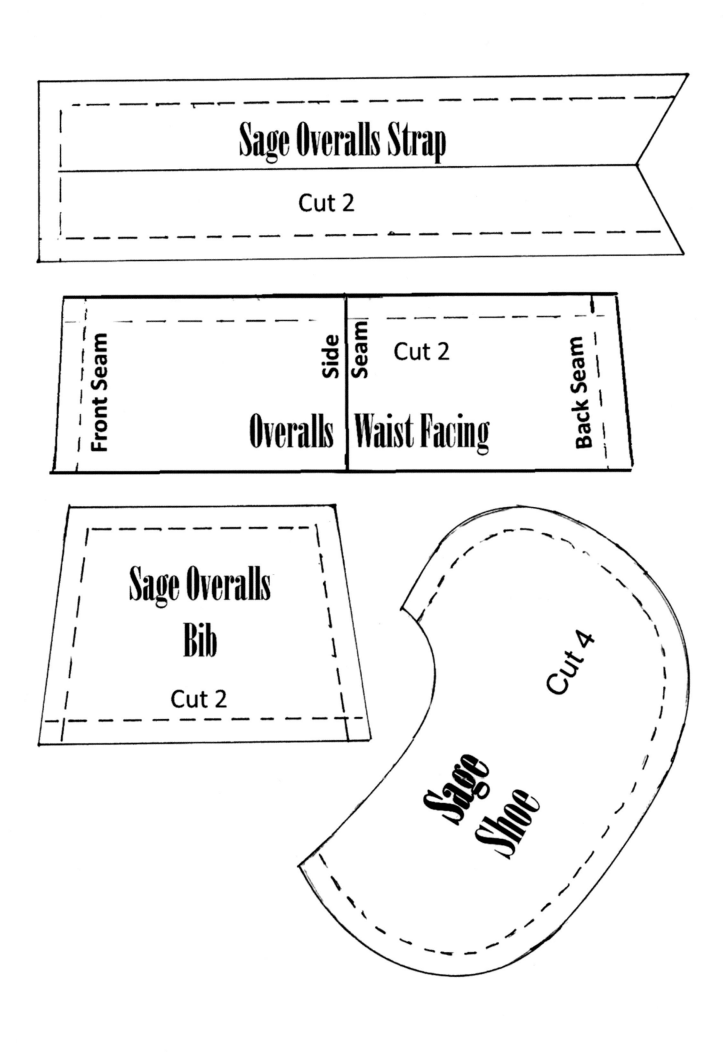

Sage Overalls Strap

Cut 2

Front Seam

Overalls

Side Seam

Cut 2

Waist Facing

Back Seam

Sage Overalls Bib

Cut 2

Sage Shoe

Cut 4

**Sage
Overalls
Front**

Cut 2

Side Seam

Center Front Seam

Attach to Overalls Front Leg here

**Sage
Overalls
Back**

Cut 2

Center Back Seam

Side Seam

Attach to Overalls Back Leg here

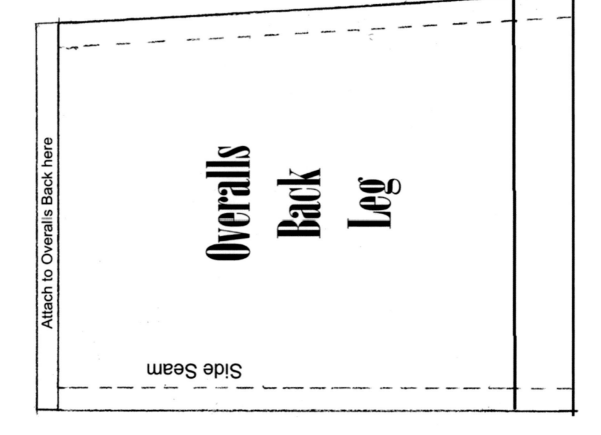

Made in the USA
Middletown, DE
08 October 2022

12204282R00020